SADDAT HASAN
MANTO

TOBA TEK SINGH
THE DOG OF TITHWAL

First published by Westland Books, a division of Nasadiya Technologies Private Limited, in 2024

No. 269/2B, First Floor, 'Irai Arul', Vimalraj Street, Nethaji Nagar, Alapakkam Main Road, Maduravoyal, Chennai 600095

Westland and the Westland logo are the trademarks of Nasadiya Technologies Private Limited, or its affiliates.

Copyright © Nasadiya Technologies Private Limited, 2024

This comic is an adaptation of two short stories by Sadat Hassan Manto—*Toba Tek Singh* and *The Dog of Tithwal*.

ISBN: 9789360453053

10 9 8 7 6 5 4 3 2 1

This is a work of fiction. Names, characters, organisations, places, events and incidents are either products of the author's imagination or used fictitiously.

All rights reserved

Book design by New Media Line Creations, New Delhi

Printed at Parksons Graphics Pvt. Ltd.

No part of this book may be reproduced, or stored in a retrieval system, or transmitted in any form or by any means, electronic, mechanical, photocopying, recording, or otherwise, without express written permission of the publisher.

TOBA TEK SINGH

"I don't want to live in either Hindustan or Pakistan. I'll live right here in this tree!"

AFTER SHOUTING FOR HOURS, THE LUNATIC FINALLY CALMED DOWN. HE CAME DOWN, EMBRACED HIS HINDU AND SIKH FRIENDS AND STARTED WEEPING.

"Please don't leave me and go to Hindustan!"

A MUSLIM M.SC.-EDUCATED RADIO ENGINEER WAS USED TO TAKING LEISURELY WALKS IN THE GARDEN, DEEP IN CONTEMPLATION. HE PREFERRED SOLITUDE AND HAD DISTANCED HIMSELF FROM THE OTHER INMATES.

ONE DAY, DISTRESSED BY ALL THIS TALK OF INDIA AND PAKISTAN ...

What are you doing? Put some clothes on.

I want to feel free. Free like Pakistan!

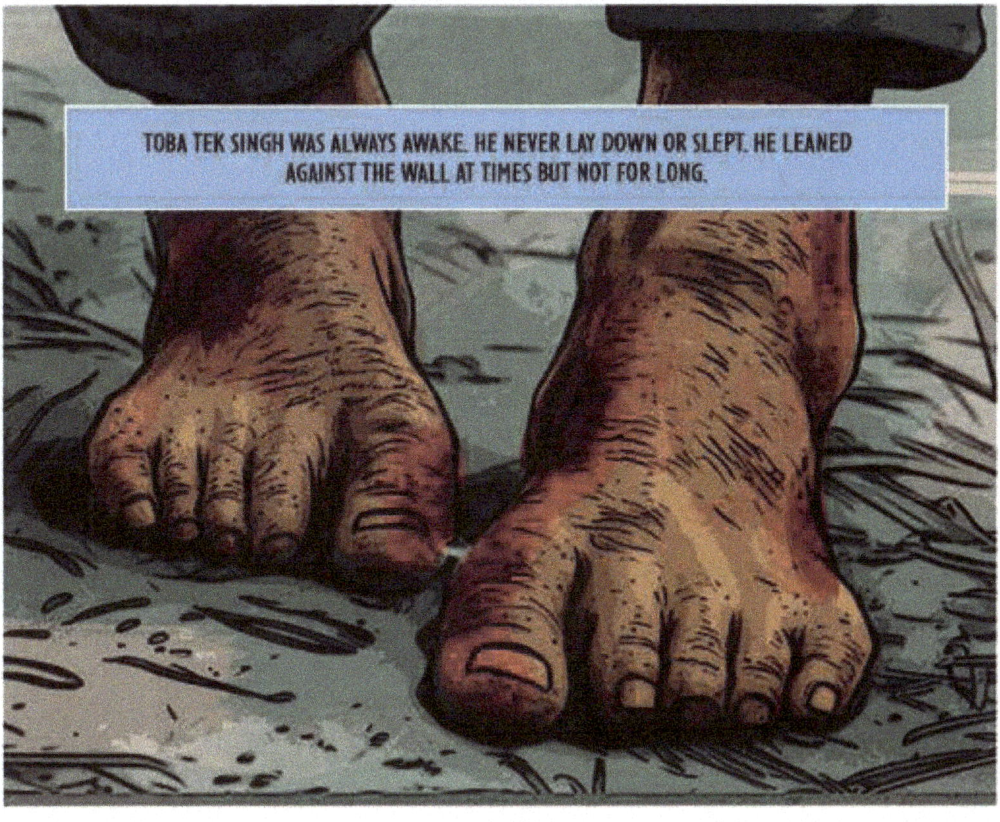

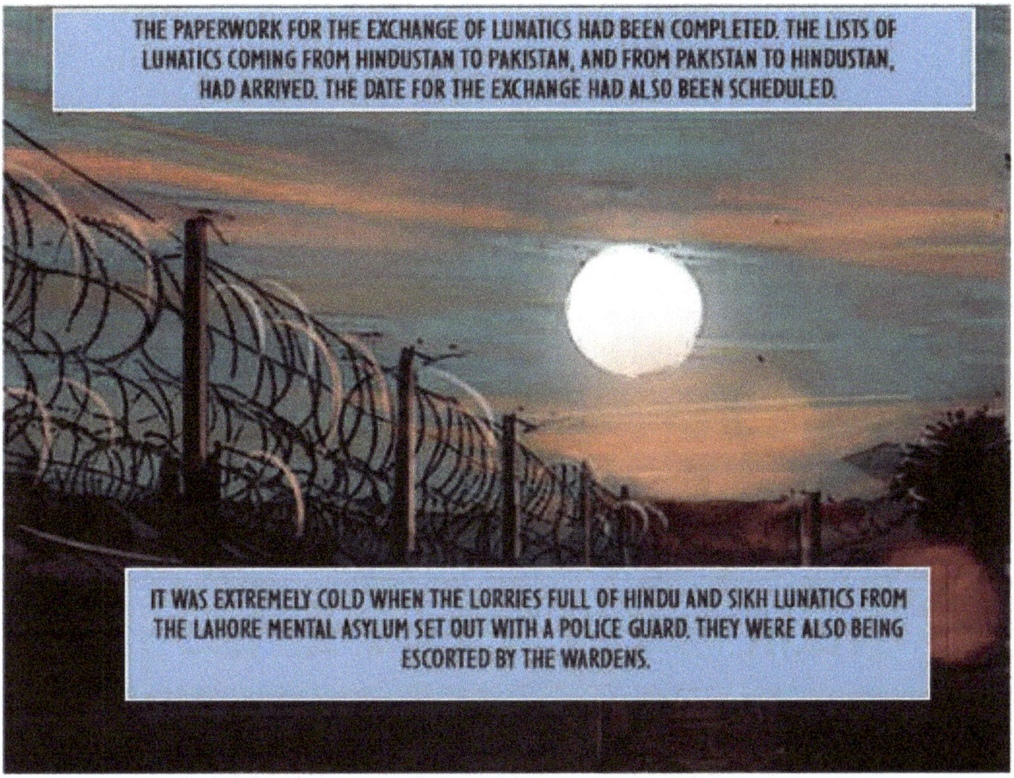

THE PAPERWORK FOR THE EXCHANGE OF LUNATICS HAD BEEN COMPLETED. THE LISTS OF LUNATICS COMING FROM HINDUSTAN TO PAKISTAN, AND FROM PAKISTAN TO HINDUSTAN, HAD ARRIVED. THE DATE FOR THE EXCHANGE HAD ALSO BEEN SCHEDULED.

IT WAS EXTREMELY COLD WHEN THE LORRIES FULL OF HINDU AND SIKH LUNATICS FROM THE LAHORE MENTAL ASYLUM SET OUT WITH A POLICE GUARD. THEY WERE ALSO BEING ESCORTED BY THE WARDENS.

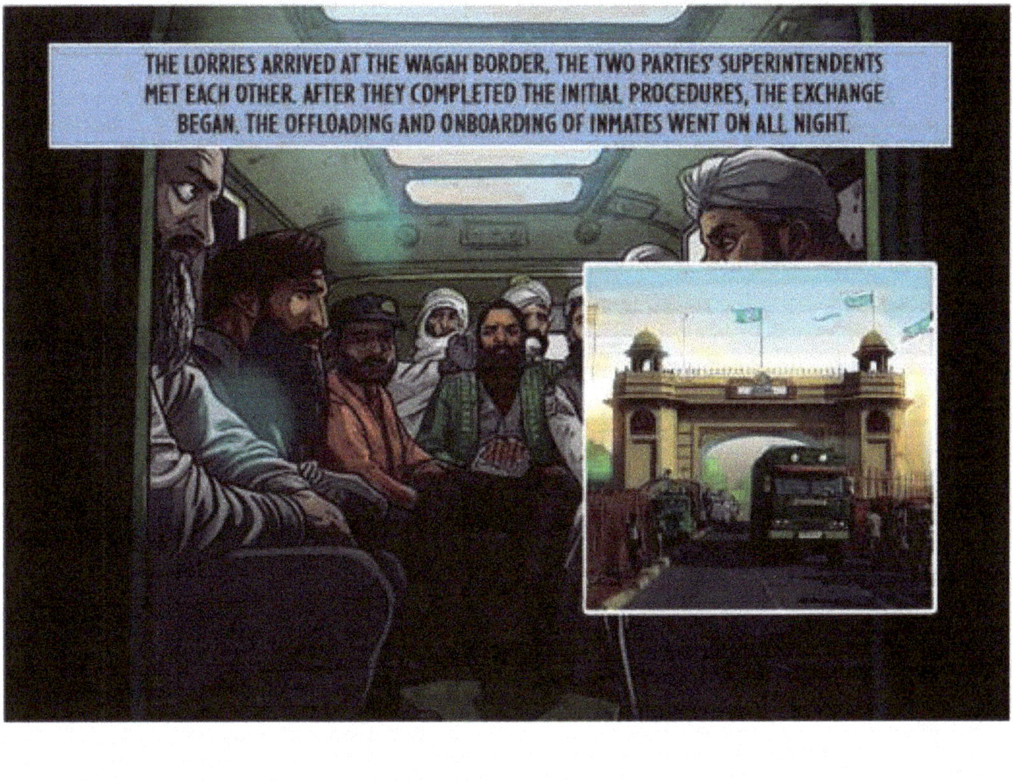

THE LORRIES ARRIVED AT THE WAGAH BORDER. THE TWO PARTIES' SUPERINTENDENTS MET EACH OTHER. AFTER THEY COMPLETED THE INITIAL PROCEDURES, THE EXCHANGE BEGAN. THE OFFLOADING AND ONBOARDING OF INMATES WENT ON ALL NIGHT.

IT WAS CHALLENGING TO REMOVE THE LUNATICS FROM THE LORRIES AND ENTRUST THEM TO THE CARE OF THE OTHER ATTENDANTS. SOME OF THEM ADAMANTLY REFUSED TO COME OUT AT ALL.

Wear these clothes.

No! I don't want to!

Let go of me!

Please calm down!

Why are you taking me away?

CRASH
CRASH

What happened?

This is the lunatic who refused to cross over.

THE DOG OF TITHWAL

> IT WAS ALMOST THE END OF SEPTEMBER, AND THE WEATHER WAS PLEASANT — NEITHER HOT NOR COLD. IT FELT AS THOUGH SUMMER AND WINTER HAD RECONCILED THEIR DIFFERENCES.

THE SOLDIERS HAD BEEN CAMPING ON THE TWO MOUNTAINS IN TITHWAL FOR SEVERAL WEEKS. THERE WAS HARDLY ANY FIGHTING EXCEPT FOR THE RITUAL OF OCCASIONALLY FIRING SOME ROUNDS.

AT NIGHT, THE SOLDIERS WOULD LIGHT HUGE FIRES AND HEAR EACH OTHER'S VOICES ECHOING THROUGH THE HILLS.

THE LAST ROUND OF TEA HAD JUST ENDED. THE FIRE HAD GONE COLD.

MOST OF THE SOLDIERS WERE ALREADY ASLEEP, BUT NOT JEMADAR HARNAM SINGH. HE WAS ON NIGHT PATROL.

RUFF RUFF

THE BARKING OF A DOG SHATTERED THE MOOD.

Where is this foolish dog's barking coming from?

RUSTLE RUSTLE

THEY HEARD SOME SOUNDS NEAR THE BUSHES ...

THE DOG BARKED AGAIN. HE SOUNDED CLOSER.

I found him behind the bushes. He told me his name was Jhun Jhun.

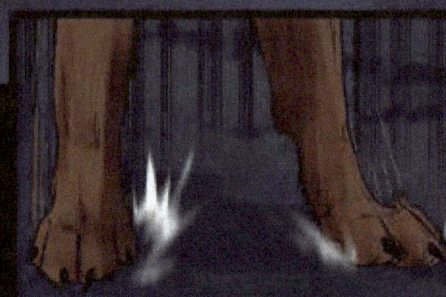

"And all Pakistanis, even dogs, will be shot."

"India Zindabad! Long live India!"

SUBEDAR HIMMAT KHAN FIRED A SHOT IN THE AIR IN RAGE, PUZZLING THE INDIAN SOLDIERS. IT WAS EARLY FOR THIS KIND OF ACTION.

BAM!

Let's give it to them.

BAM BAM

THE TWO SIDES EXCHANGED FIRE FOR HALF AN HOUR, WHICH OF COURSE WAS A COMPLETE WASTE OF TIME.

BAM BAM

FINALLY, JEMADAR HARNAM SINGH ORDERED THAT ENOUGH WAS ENOUGH.

THE BULLET HIT SOME ROCKS CLOSE TO WHERE THE DOG WAS. HE STOPPED.

TUCK TUCK

WHEN SUBEDAR HIMMAT KHAN LOOKED THROUGH HIS BINOCULARS, HE SAW THAT THE DOG HAD TURNED ROUND AND WAS RUNNING BACK.

The End

www.ingramcontent.com/pod-product-compliance
Lightning Source LLC
LaVergne TN
LVHW061626070526
838199LV00070B/6591